My My My Life

Alasdair Paterson

MY MY MY LIFE

Shearsman Books

First published in the United Kingdom in 2021 by
Shearsman Books Ltd
PO Box 4239
Swindon
SN3 9FN

Shearsman Books Ltd Registered Office
30–31 St. James Place, Mangotsfield, Bristol BS16 9JB
(this address not for correspondence)

www.shearsman.com

ISBN 978-1-84861-752-0

ACKNOWLEDGEMENTS
With thanks to the editors of *Litter*, *Long Poem Magazine*,
Molly Bloom and *Shearsman*, in which many of these first appeared;
and to Peter Hughes of Oystercatcher Press, who bought out
My life as a mad king as a pamphlet in 2016.

'My life on a meander' was developed from the author's share
of a joint project with Tilla Brading.

Cover illustration by Alys Paterson.

CONTENTS

For my family

My life as a Pict

Pict is beyond you Pict is out of bounds Pict is back there in the fern-shadow daub in the blue-dapple pine waiting for a legion

School: schooling: schooled. The portico was Athens of the North but the shadows were Roman. With certain local features, such as school houses soundly in the classical tradition but named for barbarous nations: Angles, Britons, Picts, Scots, King Kenneth Macalpine's fusion quartet. I was a Pict. I was there to be absorbed. I was there to disappear. I was there to lose my language. Not Leith but Lethe.

Pict is the weave of absence the riddle guessed by ramparts the language of bitten tongue Pict is water on the carved rock when snakes ripple and boars rush and a few words flicker words or parts of words like sword sparks or plough spray or smuts from a hearth or names for the vanished headland till the stone dries and calms

Not only/but also; either/or; unless/then. There was balance in the dominie's tough prescriptions, a blueprint for a world of certain consequences, of triumphal chariots you could ride on or trail behind in chains. *Unless*: in his hands he hefted more than a shape; there was Caesar's skull, chalk dust made palpable. And from the depths of his robe, the leather, the sanction, the shining, forked, thunderous end-of-the-matter *then*.

but Pict is across the scentless river and far from the scratch snarl bite loosed from porticos from cloisters Pict is words snagged in the memory Pict is the secret paths the night walking Pict is inside Pict is inside Pict is inside

My life with the pirates

Flag

What colours? To sail under? There's a question or two. Old salts favour the multiple choice, best kept in a flag locker snug as gunpowder, to be run up the mast at transmission time. Clue: the message is the mayhem. No codebook required. Our minimum recommendation:

> *The hourglass ultimatum*
> *Anti-coagulant red*
> *The compromised anatomy*
> *Black spot bat flap*
> *Crossed instruments of torture*
> *The jolly event horizon*

Plank

Timber, shivering. Fastidiousness of swabbed decks. Weapons to sharpen. Pressure to relieve. And always the sea, element we're on and out of, unaccountable, our bosom enemy. To propitiate.

So a rule change, a refinement in the game of wooden walls, after *stand by to repel*, after *strike your colours*. Bring it on, the loser's shaky forfeit, a one-way passage out, extruded claw of ship-substance that dangles, drops for sport, deeper than plummets sound, down and deep as krakens sleep. Or so they say.

No hope of an escape for them, no surfacing again, except in your dreams, in the breathing spaces between your dreams. Here they come, all the plungers you watched the water gulp and swallow, come specially to you, breathless to share discoveries, their buried treasure. Shells and bones, mate. Bygones. Be bygones.

Dice

A throw of loaded dice will abolish chance. But don't push your luck.

Treasure

How rich the language promises to make us, wealth come by hard or easy. We'll spend it like sailors ashore. It smells of blood, it tastes of metal, it weighs down the scales. Life-enhancing, life-destroying. Life-altering, surely.

This is the deep structure of that word-hoard, that glitter surface of thesaurus. Eight reales make one peso; pieces of eight, pure raucous silver. Clink. Eight escudos make one doubloon, golden as landfall dreams. Clink. Add sequins and moidres and pistoles and guineas for ballast, value calculable but incidence smaller. Clink. Therefore the sum (pieces of eight + doubloons + sequins + moidres + pistoles + guineas + assorted jewels + random silver and gold plate) = one dead man's chest, where x is his mark, where x is his status, where $x$bones rule, where x is not the only chromosome, where x marks the spot. Though a fistful of sand is a more usual outcome.

Parrot

Pirate. Parrot. Most letters in common. Some genes in common. Life expectancy: put your money on the parrot. Souls: keep your doubloons in your pocket.

Pirate. Parrot. A thing of shred and scratch, of excerpt and sample. Is there an echo here? Something at your shoulder, on your shoulder, tonight and every night in the cabaret of the shoulder, condensing lives to a few jaunty phrases, putting even yours in sardonic quotation marks. Speaking your life weight.

Accounting for the dead, or those about to be. Pirate. Parrot. Pierrot. Pieces of eight.

Black spot
The disc of paper, blackened on one side. The date of your death, very soon, on the other. As tipped into your hand by an old shipmate. Who else?

Open your fist again. What's there? The shadow of the earth slicing away the moon. The maw of the well with the longest drop. The banshee's open mouth. The watch-dial that needs no numbers. The coin on a dead eye. The dark smudge on the X-ray, or this slow obliteration of the sun above you as you scurry away from what comes tap-tapping down a darkening road, the birds fallen silent.

My life as a former person

Welcome to the bar of former people. You'll find us here most nights. It's a home from home, for the likes of us. More homely, if anything. No knock at the door. And if I say, I was someone once – well, weren't we all, in here? It's congenial, in a manner of speaking, to a way of thinking...

Here's all about the manner of, the way of. We speak and think, therefore. That world outside, the cold, vexing place we say is just not what it was, and the way it was, yes, when we were someone, that's everything we have to talk about. Lucky that the topic's inexhaustible. We never lose the thread. We could go on and on. We do. Stories we've told before, ten times, a hundred times, make the building blocks of evenings we've lived before, ten times, a hundred times, and they grow too, these stories, stretching out like the best do to keep us on our toes, to pick up more and more of the shoogly detritus from the back of our minds, the fragments pulled in by the magnetic force of the need to recollect correctly, to reconstruct each someone who's been someone.

We might as well be drinking embalming fluid, we may in fact be drinking embalming fluid, there's no sell-by date for that here. We could be interested in today's deal on bitter. There's usually one. We've seen it all and it was better, once. No rush to drink up and be gone. Not while we can still taste that world outside a little, between sips. Wormwood. Ashes. Gun metal. We'll build the stories up between us, building to The Story, the composite that gets it all 360 degrees. Our lives and times. The story that each of us secretly longs to see and still hopes will never be complete. Because then, what?

Pull up a chair. There's always someone who won't be back. From out there. It's not safe, you know. Now, we assume you must be here for a reason. Do we know you from somewhere? From before? Are you one of the blamed, the forsaken, the forgotten? Are you in fact a bona fide former person? You were someone once, you say. We know, we know. Weren't we all, in here?

My life as a mad king (1)

Villanelle the first

Father was a lance rampant
they say his helmet was his home
mother was a purse couchant

Lance purse ship of fools
my escutcheon word to the wise
father was a loaded spear

Churn bric-a-brac in a sea of blood
for stormy days in the alembic
mother wore her jewels to bed

Physicians heralds alchemists
swirled my flask of hand-me-downs
father was a cocked shaft

Lance purse ship gules
they held above the red red flame
mother was a stash akimbo

And saw what fused together there
the royal me the cankered swimmer
father was a lance rampant
mother was a purse couchant

Villanelle the second

My state is a broken music
it leaks leaks in shiver descants
from oubliettes and listening tubes

My tuning is dog-whistle overtone
of stifled stifling below stairs
my sustain is mandrake rendition

Acclaimed my humalong masterwork
lachrimae of smiles and pincers
dungeon stone what a good ear

Fetch the parchment rule the staves
string notes out on the sounding rack
my rosin is scarified minstrel

Virtuoso on a ground of flesh
I peeled redacted lamentations
from garderobes and palace spies

So straggle in the detuned consort
for palm court broadcasts to the nation
my state is a broken music
from oubliettes and listening tubes

Villanelle the third

Her face flickered flared
evening's candle when
a page turns in the music.

Or town square spark and catch
under a choice of heretic flesh
her tongue flicked flashed

Or an ember's appetite
when the glass kiln feeds
her mirage preened in the mirror

At the ball the ball of burning men
she hid me in her skirts
her thighs flexed fused

Wildwood masquers melted faster
than their own ardent torches
an outrage by the tinder muses

I felt the heat sweep past
felt my poor heart turn to glass
her face flickered flared
a page turned in the music

Villanelle the fourth

My state is broken music
my station is broadcast mondegreen
my stanza is breakdown miserere

My stagecraft is brutality masquerade
my statement is brimstone miniscule
my state is broken music

My stairwell is breathless mantrap
my stagnation is bridewell miasma
my stanza is breakdown miserere

My standard is braggadocio mystique
my standpoint is breastplate mountebank
my state is broken music

My statuary is bricolage mausoleum
my starchart is braille metamorphosis
my stanza is breakdown miserere

My stalker is brainstorm martyrdom
my status is bravura maelstrom
my state is broken music
my stanza is breakdown miserere

Villanelle the fifth

I am looking in the glass
and I am looking from the glass
and that is not me looking

That one won't quite do won't do
laggard mops and sluggard mows
I am looking in the mirror

Nice tailoring wrong dummy
my tapestry his heresy
and that is not me looking

We stare past each other's stare
I see his bunch of shadows
I am at the looking glass

We tried to open this door skin
our palm prints went unrecognised
and that is not me looking

That one thinks he really is
and I am not quite not sure
I am looking in the glass
and this is not me looking

Villanelle the sixth

A pandemonium of smoke and fire
a panoply of wine and roses
a pantomime of flesh and blood

A panjandrum of cap and bells
a pantaloon of shreds and patches
a pandemonium of court and spark

A panpipe of pomp and circumstance
a panorama of nature and nurture
a pantomime of blood and iron

A panzer of spark and misfire
a panegyric of fragments and ruins
a pandemonium of death and taxes

A panache of thrust and parry
a pander of mouth and trousers
a pantomime of flesh and grass

A pandemic of pipe and slippers
a pantheon of air and angels
a pandemonium of ashes and diamonds
a pantomime of flesh and glass

My life as a wordsmith

Word, some class of a word, a word of sorts, and it came to me, let's just be clear, came of its own accord, off its own bat, a word with presence, no enticements necessary, no entrapments, that must be stressed, no trawling the word-bars, not this time, no prising open the word-hoard, no deployment of press-gang or word-hounds, it came to me, over the welcome mat, through the ever-open door, the chance you give, the risk you take, and it was brimful with possibility, the kind of word you could bite on, the sort of word you could build on, no wonder I spent the day, all day with it, tried to put things right for it, as right as could be, poor complicated word, some class of a word yoke, I've had worse days, worse days altogether with a word, though words are draining, of course, matter of record, a bit of a trial, that wearing sense of entitlement, that high-maintenance imperiousness, that completely irritating, endearing lack of self-knowledge, must stress that it came to me, I didn't go looking, people are needy but words are needier, it's on the record, not that it didn't play hard to get, not that it didn't struggle and wriggle and frick and frack and shape-shift and shilly-shally, a word all right, to the very vanishing-point of its ink, to the very edge of darkness of its pixels, to the last rusting wire of its border with silence,

not your ordinary word, not to me, an impact, immediate, felt it there and then, so I stunned it with a handy best of intentions, it went quieter, held it down, stay there, I tipped out other words, boxed away for such moments, there they stood, trying to get ready for their close-up, blinking and startled, some manifestly, magnificently useless, some amazingly, impressively apt, I hummed and hawed and finicked, made my choices, offered them up, swapped them round, fixed them with a filigree, medusa coil behind the scenes, discreet clank of restraints, a chorus-line chain-gang of harmony and dissonance, smell of lightning strike, no loose ends, no leakages, and there it was, poem with the word embedded, no less than it deserved, the word reset, the word rebooted, burnished in certain of its meanings, disabled in certain of its former associations, a thing of shimmers and shadows only I'd spotted, yoked to its chosen company, I was pleased enough, studied it from all angles, needed to be sure,

then came the exhibit, then the broadcast, then the tour, the Word Tour, the Word and the Words Tour, the Look What A Word I Found Tour, pleased with the poem, pleased with the word in its matrix, pleased with myself, but futile of course, the word was already out there in its millions, so many millions of it, all doing something a little different, all promising to be your own, your very own unique copy, but just look at it here, the poem with the word, that's my own work, my poem, yours now too if you like, look at the word in the poem, the one that came to me, as it trembles, as it flickers, as it hisses like water in a smithy, as it coos like a dove in the cage of the hand, as it shines like a taper to the outer room, a cut moonstone of a word, though sometimes it feels the pull, the pain of its losses, its phantom meanings, must stress it came to me, my own unique copy now, could be yours too, yours only a little bit different, that's understood, just turn the page if you tire of it, I do, often keep it shut away, like to remember it just as it came at first, some class of a word, another wordsmith might have thought twice, I always think three times, it's not enough, I think I'm done with it now, thank goodness, put it away, let it gather dust, never want to see it again, I think I'll just take another look

My life on the run

I'm under investigation in that town I wrote. It's not what it was, back in the day, but then, what is? An arrest, announce the latest bulletins, is imminent. No surprise that the streets tonight are silence stretched next to silence, like strings no-one dares to strum for fear of the wrong music. My people have slipped inside themselves, barred the door, taken a light to a shuttered room. There's not a word to be heard about me, which says it all to the trained ear.

A car slows, engine cut, lights extinguished; the top agent, best man for the job, deft, implacable, torch and weapon in capacious pockets, is out and about in my street plan. He has the scent all right, though I've had long enough for my precautions: safe suburb, safe flat, safe beard, safe decade.

This dilapidated end of town is promising, I imagine him thinking. I sense the scrutiny of a man who's seen it all before. Who senses me. The notebook's out. Weathered statue, pointing, loaf in hand – the father? Overgrown floral clock, name still distinct in alpines – the mother? Plaque outside the shuttered Road To Ruin Inn – the brother? Even a children's playground, deserted at this hour…

He's purposeful now, the direction unerring, getting close. Torchlight and footsteps cross the courtyard, pause by the puddle that reflects half-remembered constellations, botched architecture. A deep breath. Closer still. A knock at the door. Bang to rights. I open it. It's me out there, as expected, but older, harder. Worn. We've got each other covered. We're not impressed.

You could have done better, we both say.

My life with the dead white males

As I was motivating up the Cork to Dublin highway, who should I spy but my father-in-law at large among the roadside picnics, big potato thumb extended. I hit the brakes fast – hard enough to make St Christopher on the mirror dance the St Vitus and the parish raffle tickets on the dashboard make a random draw (first prize: a brand-new combine harvester; second prize: the hamburger-van concession by the weeping statue; third prize: a week with the flagellant order of your choice). He climbed in, still with that Hollywood smile. He said: *How are things in Port Sunlight?* I said: *The Wirral is everything that is the case.* I said: *Jim, we all thought you were dead.* He said: *Only in a manner of speaking.*

As I was swimming with the ease of a young gazelle down the River Mersey, hardly distinguishable from the great grey-green greasy Limpopo apart from Liver Birds snacking on orchids and the flotsam of Stratocasters, my brother at the Pier Head in full military fig (King's African Rifles) proffered his swagger stick to help me out. This was unexpected. Says I: *What's with the uniform then, Davy?* Says he: *I wear it for its proven climatic advantages and for the regimental motto: You Never Drown In The Same River Twice.*

As I was labouring up Arthur's Seat, amusing myself with haiku misshapes like –

> *In a minute*
> *when I get my breath*
> *back, the famous view.*

– my father joined me for the final stretch, tacking between gorse and basalt on a moonless night. The famous view was

Edinburgh, our city, like a computer etherised upon a table, lid prised off to reveal that old-time Calvinist binary, *light* or *not light, right* or *very fucking wrong, pal.* He was checking if I'd lost my sense of humour, seeing I'd scattered his ashes here from an extinct volcano and never got the joke. Me: *Things got a bit black there for a while. And I did worry where your ashes might fetch up.* Him: *That was fine, apart from the speck that went into a mutton pie at Raith Rovers. Don't worry, Aly. It's always darkest just before the Scottish Enlightenment . Moreover, a scattering of the ashes will never abolish chance.*

My turn at the oracle business soon enough. I'll try to remember: good intentions, something Delphic. The rest is up to the next batch.

My life as a mad king (2)

Villanelle the seventh

Winter is winter comes winter
a storming of the paradise
too cold a grip can crack you

Rook banners pincer movements
trenching tools and covert ops
winter is age comes winter

Parterre provocations quelled
rosebeds put to the question
too cold a grip can crack you

When trees embrace their inner ghosts
your mirror mists with unknown knowns
winter is love turns winter

Turn loose the blazing dancers
break out the sun god tapestries
too cold a grip can crack you

Summer gasps for the fountain
autumn shames the alchemist
winter is winter comes winter
too cold a grip can crack you

Villanelle the eighth

Late nights spying on the spies
rats' nests and covert ops discuss
dark lantern check eyes hooded check

Marvel as they palm the ace
gasp at the skin they flay from truth
night eases my spyholes open

Their tongues sidle round my name
some words burn your mouth like pitch
candles eavesdrop on the listeners

Mankind's proper study is
the twitch that thrills the spider's web
black hours coaxing black harvests

Clouds are swagged across the moon
someone's been talking in their sleep
embers dowsed and hands on knives

Doctors failed to break my code
the fool stole my cipherbook
dead silence grows death letters
coins gleam like the roots of pyres

Villanelle the ninth

Dark as six feet of dungeon earth
spidery as a signed confession
silent as cloaks by the frozen fountain

Well-hung as the family tree
doleful as dinner with parasites
dark as the assassin's night shift

Abysmal as two steps off the map
dazzling as first dip in the grimoire
silent as a street of burnt books

Scarlet as a fistful of roses
white as the lips of the food taster
dark as the black supper reveal

Jumpy as a court painter's eyelid
sleek as a specialist in royal blood
silent as a nun's heart burial

False as false as teeth and smiles
true as my last word on the subject
dark as six feet of dungeon earth
silent as steel by the frozen fountain

Villanelle the tenth

My gardens grow with iliads
I sing short triumphs rough endings
odysseys of flight and pounce

Puffed up jumped up blood up jut
of breast and straight for the eyes
my gardens groom iliads

Or a talon's worth of grip
on the things that pass for knowledge
odysseys of flinch and pincer

Or offerings to the goddess
scats of skin and claw and bone
my gardens groan with iliads

Learn patience for whatever comes
crumbs or the soft head dropping them
odysseys of fang and pinion

Better to soar and scan and swoop
than be judged in the dark corner
my gardens grow with iliads
odysseys of flight and pounce

Villanelle the eleventh

A banquet greased by beggars
a glass with added glass
a saucerful of secrets

A farthingale crammed with frankincense
a codpiece rammed with cod
a banquet grazed by bankers

A locket drenched in lachrimae
a joint spiced with jacquerie
a saucerful of sanctitas

A honeycomb aglow with hives
a trencher agroan with trauma
a banquet garnished with butchers

A mouth clenched on misereres
a doublet sewn with deathmasks
a saucerful of serpents

A pie stuffed with pincushions
a rack primed with ribs
a banquet greased by beggars
a saucerful of secrets

Villanelle the twelfth

Go little poems get some help
some watch mending some stitch in time
no future jingle jangling freestyle

An adept of the abacus
would know how many beats make four
go little poems get an audit

For tangled fleece call the shearsman
uncut hedge fetch a ladder boy
no topiary no style

Bedside manners lull you lull you
then bring up the hungry leeches
go little poems get some treatment

A measured trip across the floor
light fantastic quick quick slow
no trophies dancing doggy style

Go little poems get some lessons
go little poems get a room
go little poems get some help
no future jingle jangling freestyle

My life in a restoration project

See me – my brilliant remark to no-one in particular – *see me, I'm back.* At least it tickled the crows; they presented me with a map of the estate rendered in echoes. The old seized-up gate still hoped it knew its duty too, after a nudge and a scrape; even the family escutcheon, hung there like a withered animal, said *welcome home, prodigal boy.*

Homecomings don't always go as you'd imagine: for example, carriage wheels mashing grass and briar, for example yews along the avenue run wild from their invisible cages. The ponds' tarnished silver, I knew that though: Granny's eyes in the landing mirror. And there loomed the house at last, a digest of my Boys' Book of Architecture (or a wormhole through it), where the last servants had been lined up – drooped and pouched, estate apples too long in the apple store.

A fire was set in the study. Father's blotchy shelves of sermons were now so dry that you could ask no better kindling. Halitosic platitudes. Flicker. Waspish strictures. Crackle. Intemperate menaces. Blaze. I always liked a fire. Then my money bags and dice went behind the secret panel and the weapons in the drawer marked *Danger.*

That painting I always hated, *The return of the prodigal?* I sold it. It cleared the debts. Promoted in its place, there's only a cack-handed daub, but what a theme – *The return of Ulysses,* with that score-settling shower of arrows. My hero. Let me describe the soundtrack too: a restorative tock-tock of shears cutting back, mousey scrape of widows' and daughters' skirts combing tremulously up the drive, the ghost of an ovation from the ancestral claque.

See me, said I, to no one in particular. And no-one in particular answered – just a pheasant coming down the park on the fidget, its cry like a key grating in a lock.

My life as a detail

When I fell down in the wood did the trees hear? Did anyone?

How long would I have needed to lie motionless, supine in the wood aforesaid, to be pronounced dead? A minute, a week or a month? A few hundred years? And then, pronounced dead by whom? By you? By an expert? Before or after the leaves cover me? Is there in fact the slightest chance of a single leaf covering me? Do leaves fall here? Am I in fact dead now? What do I mean by 'fact'? What do I mean by 'now'? Is this a deathly pallor or leaf dapple? Or is the paint ageing, changing, though so much more slowly than flesh would?

Shall we go forward on the shared understanding that I really am dead? Shall we assume that understanding is something we can really share? Can we retain the word 'really', with all its dubious, head-scratching applicability, for the time being? What is the time with you, by the way? Am I in time and if so what time?

How do you die in a wood? In my own time, i.e. in the time herein represented? Shall we consider homicide? The footpad stealthy? The cuckold enraged? The war party past caring? The lunatic, terrified and terrible? The family, as usual? Or mishap, perhaps? The tree root? The fallen bough? The passing boar? The lightning strike? Should we not consider natural causes various? The whole unknown mechanism within, shuddering to a standstill, heart, brain, lungs, failing in a wood? Should we not suspect judicial issues or similar? The squeal at the end of the manhunt? Gurgle and twitch till the bough breaks? Is self-harm, alas, a legitimate line of enquiry? What about divine judgement? Does it exist? If so, does it cover all of the above? If not, can I blame the artist?

What do I look like? Is this a good colour? Can we blame the light through the green leaves? Do you agree, it doesn't look good for me? Supine, white hair, eyes staring upward? Can you see me, now? Who else do you think will see me? The peasant and his horse, perhaps they'll see me next, as they plough a furrow in the direction of the wood? The shepherd who notices nothing, not even his sheep, but might hear a cry of discovery? In a moment? The fisherman distracted by a big ripple? The ships sailing on? Everyone who misses everything, even the tangle of legs and wings and estuary water out there?

You didn't miss that fall, though, did you? The watery one? At least, not the moment of impact? Wasn't it intended you would notice? The title being a clue? *The Fall of Icarus*? Or maybe *Landscape with the the Fall of Icarus*? Doesn't that get you looking? And the artistic framing that leads your eye there eventually? The splash you see, that no-one in the picture sees? Being the point about suffering? That no-one sees? But who notices me, here, lying in a wood? Did you really notice? How many times did you look before you noticed? Did you get a tip-off? About looking for the hidden meaning, the same meaning as the splash everyone in the picture misses, but a meaning you missed too? The real meaning? In a blind spot, in the corner of a scene, in a wood?

So will the plough-horse discover me in a second? Will he shy away? Will the proverbs rise like bones from the glistening furrows? The careless shepherd dreams while his sheep stray? The plough doesn't stop just because a man dies? About suffering they were never wrong, the old masters?

My life as a mad king (3)

Villanelle the thirteenth

Of unmade kings there's no end
here come the angry horsemen
here come the purifiers

Before the chrism licks your scalp
send off the stranglers with a list
no end of kings who never quite

Keep your friends on subsidy
keep your enemies subsoil
here come the pacifiers

Step away from parapets
no shut-eye in locked libraries
of misshelved kings there's no end

Up the food tasting budget
set a guard to watch the guard
here come the paramedics

Wave your sons off to the wars
ransom what a long slow business
of unmade kings there's no end
here come the purifiers

Villanelle the fourteenth

Madness id est noble rot
let me let me count the ways
bloodlines and/or events dear boy

Deep down in the escutcheon
a blot a spot a blisterette
madness id est noble rot

Or some things the elders did
shadowlands behind closed doors
bloodlines and/or events dear boy

My shelves bow with case histories
each worm is a perfect digest
madness id est noble rot

Read all about the greenwood loon
the poster boy for love philtres
bloodlines and/or events dear boy

The one who burned his playhouse down
the one who failed to read the wall
madness id est noble rot
bloodlines and/or events dear boy

Villanelle the fifteenth

The planet spins me through the dark
my cosmos is blacker than yours
I never ask for signs of grace

I fought the wars of missing gods
my god is more absent than yours
the planet turns me to the dark

In the banned book library
my worms are better read than yours
I never looked for signs of grace

New worlds wear my livery
my germs are better armed than yours
the planet sneezes through the dark

My sins fill up a box a day
my soul floats lighter than yours
I never lack for signs of grace

My winding sheet stays under wraps
my shelf life is longer than yours
the planet spins me through the dark
I never ask for signs of grace

Villanelle the ultimate

Threescore years and ten go past
and seventy-one won't be back
and even the fool turned white

Many a truth lurks in jestbooks
but not enough to fill the cracks
threescore years and ten trudge past

Riddle me sir which came first
the neck-wringing or the omelette
and even the jester blanched

To teach the answer to what goes
on four and two and three legs
threescore years and ten grind past

Teeth and bells and cap and smiles
a song or two about the rain
and even the zany tottered

A man walks into an oubliette
I forget what happens next
forget what happens next
forget

Villanelle the ultimate and

Crack
head
forget

Windows
fire
crack

Corridors
stairwells
forget

Blood
steel
crack

Word
song
forget

Father
moth mother moth
crack
forget

My life *au contraire*

To trudge head down onwards ever onwards or sink down on the memorial bench with the celebrated view just as darkness falls.

To be observably balding or detectably bewigged. To be mutton dressed as lamb or mutton dressed as *mouton*. To bridle at the term 'curmudgeon' or bite its hand off.

To be innocuous to the blurry point of invisibility or sashay out as a ready-made pin-sharp figure of fun. To buy cartons of the soups you actually prefer or those you can actually open. To take the bait or bite the lip.

To obsess about the Queen's English going to the dogs or smile to think how many years it is since one was favoured with a glimpse of, like, yer actual royal corgi, ken whit ahm sayin pal. To cosy up in bed imagining wage-slave ex-colleagues trudging workwards through the rain or get up anyway because standards must be maintained. To refuse the can of worms or rejoice that it does exactly what it says on the tin.

To respect the right to remain silent or show it the instruments of torture. To pimp the engine of slow draggy days or stamp stamp stamp fruitlessly on the brakes. To grieve over your shrinking stock of bosom buddies or rejoice that your imaginary friend is back after all these years.

To take pleasure in family photo albums or be grateful that, for your most vivid memories, no negatives exist. To tell a lie and disappoint an angel or tell the truth and spoil the joke. To make up your mind not to die wondering or sort of feel it's wondering gets you through the day.

To ply charity shops with all the seminal works you'll have no time to read again or find comfort in calculating how many decades it should take to get through all the unread books from the same shops now piled high on the stairs. To get into e-books because therein lies the future or remain convinced that the contours of your personality are best mapped by the titles and editions and colours and inscriptions and marginalia and stains and gaps and general wear and tear on your shelves. To favour the future tense because it works or because it will only work for a while.

To drop everything and just go – or check all the switches first and wonder about making sandwiches. To pride yourself on the crispness of your memories or on the clarity of your conviction that whatever you remember isn't likely to have been that way at all. To remain a fan of the words "happily ever after" or concede that they are comprehensively undermined by the words "funeral plan".

To maintain as an article of faith that the stairs must have a top and a bottom or voice your suspicion that the prison might be infinite. To be moved by the spiritual import of the central panel of the triptych or more impressed by the colour harmonies and the rendering of the drapery. To feel a glow at how awfully nice it's going to be among the saved souls in the left-hand panel or allow the thought to cross your mind that after-life in the right-hand panel looks, by comparison, pretty damn lively.

To encounter in the mirror the furrowed lineaments of accumulated wisdom or the air coming out of an old balloon. To be satisfied that all those regrettable compromises were necessarily part of the strategy to change the system from within, or just a little guilty that the smokescreen of system change allowed you to enjoy all the fruits of these compromises. To buy into the notion that human evolution is driving us into a world of new possibilities or, on empirical evidence, beyond the viability of our teeth.

To be borne away on the currents of Renaissance polyphony or feel increasingly unembarrassed that the soundtrack of your life was, is and ever shall be cheap music. To dismay the family with ill-considered proposals for the comeback tour or inappropriate quips about guid tunes played on auld fiddles. To tease the children with plans to spend their inheritance or get on with spending it and let them find out later.

To feel the need to cling to the guard-rail or the urge to set foot on the space beyond just because. To stare into glass after filled glass hoping your face will eventually surface or slowly submerge. To reach out and touch life with your old confidence or be embarrassed by how cold your hands are these days.

To try again and fail again or think it may be easier all round to establish a more generous definition of success. To conclude that what doesn't kill you makes you stronger or, on reflection, stranger. To watch sleeplessly as night turns into day, as a condemned man waits hoping at least that the last breakfast will be up to scratch, or come to groggily in a susurration of dispersing dreams like a castaway washed up in the surf.

To deduce that it was Colonel Mustard in the conservatory with the candlestick or your parents in the lounge with the White Heather Club. To go out to the bluebell wood for a stocktake of your life or decide that one life is not long enough to account for this rock, this rivulet, these flowers, this dance of leaves. To lie under a hedge pondering whether to make your indelible contribution to regional poetry with 'The man with the blue tractor' or with '13 ways of eating a blackbird'.

To experience an epiphany of sorts re the title of the final volume of your autobiography: 'Over the hill: or at least somewhere thereabouts I seem to remember, but I could be wrong, hmm'. To climb into bed exhilarated by a good day getting your long-nourished book project underway or admit as darkness falls that the title really says it all. To face the fact that your style all along has been grappa with a dash of curaçao or Kurosawa with a dash of Capra.

To deplore the cruelties of the Roman arena or dream a little dream about which of your contemporaries you might send out across the bloody sand like Orpheus, armed only with a harp, to charm the wild beasts. To back the proposition that about suffering they were never wrong, the old masters, or wonder whether being eaten and excreted by something beaky throughout eternity can really still be part of the Church's teaching. To congratulate yourself that, like an oyster, you produced the pearl that is your family, or have an inkling that your family is more inclined to see you as the piece of grit.

To despair when your favourite pétanque shot, the high lob with side-spin, puts your back out, or feel a certain smugness at having incurred a sports-related injury. To look forward to another twenty years behind the wheel or acknowledge that if you were your passenger you'd be fidgeting with that door-handle too. To be convinced that your investigations are bringing you closer to an understanding of the universe and your place in it, or to an acceptance that your life and the universe have been, in their varying degrees, a great waste of time.

To support with pride the myriad developments and improvements transforming your home city or feel wistful that the silhouette of its skyline and the graph of your brainwaves are becoming quite divergent. To say that nothing can come out of nothing or decide to say nothing. To bob around happily in the amniotic fluid of nostalgia broadcasting or suffer nightmares in which the celebrity undead of yesteryear crawl jerkily out of the TV set.

To like nothing better than to linger by the window in the last hour of the day – or close the curtains uneasily, reflecting that, where an estate is haunted, a window is just another turn of the screw. To go out to the hazel wood because a fire is in your head or on a quest for evidence that the Ordnance Survey has been infiltrated by psychogeographers. To be in two minds as to whether you might have been happier as a free man in Paris or a fireman on Harris.

To view the veteran maverick politician with an increasing weariness or continue to give him the benefit of the doubt, especially since you're so often mistaken for him in public these days. To take after your father in his ability to make a garden or your grandfather in his ability to make a garden and move house. To launch another search-and-destroy mission among the flower beds or finally appreciate that nothing there is as compelling as the languorous depredations of snails.

To give away all your material possessions and move to a mountain hut for indefinite moon-viewing and composition of short verses, wine glass in hand, or calculate in mid-clearance that among the bric-a-brac you've been accumulating for sixty years there must surely be some items worth a good wee bit in the collectables market. To decide that your next and maybe last work will be called 'Closing oppositions or 70 dilemmas to resolve before you die'. To discover on a recount that it will have to be called 'Closing oppositions or 62 dilemmas to resolve before you die'.

To trudge head down onwards ever onwards or, you know what, just stop here.

My life on a meander

1.

They waved goodbye
I waved back
and so on and so forth

It was the best
of their leaving presents
the truest way
of measuring a road
where x is the total
of final scenes
the sum of angry rooms
and pindrop cafés
pavement performances
of smiles and handkerchiefs
and neon no regrets
on the edge of town
where cars accelerate away
and drivers sink back
sink back at last
and let elsewhere do its work

I waved back
I liked my present
and the bend in the road
couldn't come soon enough

2.

Then it was
that time of year
to think about roads
and map contours
springing up
like paper sculpture
and goodbye

Then it was
that time of year
everything round me
familiar but brightened
brighter than ever
and did I really
want to go
and I would I would
and goodbye

Then it was
that time of year
orchard grass
and cool bottles
the sway of a neck
and that feel of
not much longer
and goodbye

Then it was
that time of year
ghost-scents
from all the gardens
I'd dug and then abandoned
and goodbye

Then it was
that time of year
leaves settled
on a dark pool
eyelids I'd closed
and goodbye

3.

In the middle of
nothing there's a house
and you wonder who
lives there what
choice was made

In the middle of
big-boned hills
or bog or suffocations
of conifer there's
always a house

There's always
someone walking past

4.

The last road was abject
pocked and slithery
through forests and
moors past hovels
past ruins to a bridge
the most abject of
bridges it trembled
if you glanced
in its direction

And the long tumultuous
drop to where the river
left the rocks
to get on with it

And the other side
as wind-torn and stony
as where we stood

She said
she'd take
the opposite direction

I said
I've already been there

I waved
from the other side

5.

By the time I got there
the fatted calf
was well-congealed
and they'd emptied
most of the bottles

No-one was very
pleased to see me
you must have missed
the path they said
you must have been
on the wrong map

Ah no I said
it was the right road
all the way

It just took longer

My life on ice

Where ice made its last stand over the river channels, they set explosives to crack and rumble downstream. I thought of the arc basso profundo makes from last judgement to your gut, or ice-breaker waves of vodka shocking loose a frosted tongue.

Then chords from an accordion fanned out in riverboat wakes to lap the feet of the birches and our captain walked the gangplank all smiles – gold, gold, gold, gold.

Down in the saloon, where words still burned recklessly, some rhapsodised about the river, all we could learn from it, how it waits steadfastly to slip its ice-shackles and wrap itself in birch. And some argued the lesson was the persistence of ice.

And me, a tribe of one, who thought they were both right and what of it? And skimmed a stone and celebrated its unlikely teeter that moment and that moment and that moment. Not forever.

My life between icebergs

Friday night in the Titanic Restaurant. Tragedy + distance = business opportunity.

We've drunk our first vodka toast ('to friendship') and made choices from the English menu. *Ice hummocks*: a calving of ravioli in clear broth. *Herring in a life jacket*: all fur coat and no ship. *Sea Bottom*: a murky mousse we'll get to eventually.

Under the trompe l'œil ceiling, a painted gash in painted metal plate with painted protrusions of flat fish (fish that are *What every woman wants*, the menu tells us), we're inevitably discussing collision courses. My turn for a toast. I praise the construction and navigation of our project, its manoeuvrability around and away from icebergs – of which there are many in international waters like ours. Tanya the translator, an ironist from birth, rolls her eyes. The shop-window dummy dressed as Leonardo Di Caprio listens impassively. A dozen glasses are raised and emptied.

Gennadi, our host, is drinking, if not like a fish, at least like a man who has to try a little harder. His resemblance to the former Party Secretary, even down to the cranial birthmark, is no longer working for him. He is sweatily engaged with our topic, which is: why did the Titanic, conjured up here with such incredibly resourceful lack of taste, sink? Going too fast through an ice-field? Faulty in its bulkhead construction? Already weakened by a fire in the coal bunker?

It sank because it hit an iceberg. A very large iceberg that no-one spotted. A very large iceberg that an unsinkable ship should still have survived a collision with. But the captain tried to avoid it, as was natural, and so the flank of the ship, not the bows, hit and was ripped. A head-on collision would have been catastrophic for those at the front of the ship, but the ship would still have floated. Or so I tell Gennadi.

He likes this. Next time, he says, when we have things sorted out, after a bit of motherland rebuilding, when we find other things to believe in and be proud of and build our lives on, next time maybe if there's an iceberg in front we'll take the hit full-on. Last time we swerved and that didn't work out so well. Incidentally, my friend, doesn't that make you the iceberg? Or was that just last time?

Here come our dishes and more bottles for more toasts. The waitresses' short skirts and matelot tops say: don't take it too seriously, and you know, we're all post-modernists now. The piranhas in the tank say: yes, but be sure to pay your bill. Remember: the ones who were in charge before, they're still in charge now. They were first into the lifeboats, carrying their valuables and other people's. They got back to business. They're unsinkable.

My life as a bridegroom

I'm serially misunderstood: a man of the world certainly, but this heart's as romantic as anyone's. I love the wooing, the wedding, all the delicious vulnerabilities of cherishing and trusting another. Can I call to mind my wedding days? All of them? Yes, distinctly, every last one. I pride myself on that. I keep them close.

Not that they didn't resemble each other. There would be early morning fuss with irreproachable tailoring, the beard-trim and the sounds of anxious scurry in the kitchen. I'd descend the castle stairs to a medley of celebratory jingling and jangling – the chapel bells would be hard at it, I'd hear the harness of the approaching wedding carriage and a counterpoint, the hefty keys swinging on my belt. Then there would be the same small chapel and the same small priest. The repeating visions of white purity and the pallor of the faces above it. The flicker of candles and the glow of flowers. Should I also mention the tremulousness of first kisses, first awkward dances, flushed withdrawals to the bridal chamber?

But yet they were all quite different, each with a unique savour – take my word as an involuntary connoisseur. For example, there would be differences in the morning light coming through the chapel windows, in the networks of age progressing across the priest's face, in the colour and shape of the eyes behind the veils, in the fit of dresses at waist and bosom, in the seasonal variation in bouquets. And, naturally, in the perfume and the taste of the never-to-be-forgotten opening kisses. I say nothing of the first nights together, being a gentleman. Well, more than just a gentleman, as we know.

What followed is even more distinctive in the memory: a particular way of wearing the hair, the wardrobe selections, the modes of sporting the entrusted keys, of tiptoeing past a certain forbidden door – a playful little temptation – and bringing life to my stone labyrinth till death us do part. Which it did, with distressing regularity; sad, the short lives of young women in this blighted era. And I'd warned them of the dangers of castle life, of illnesses and accidents, warned them till we were both blue in the face, till nothing remained but to find the same momentous door ajar, call in the tame doctor and the tame priest and make the usual funeral arrangements – private, closed casket.

Forgive me – you've heard more than enough about my tragedies. Except to add that for you, for us, they've created opportunities. Sir, it's in my mind to marry again and I seek a young woman who will be a good fit for this stage of my life. Have you guessed? Of course, I wish to woo your daughter – that is, woo you for your daughter. And if I spread out my many sweet nothings, which might catch your fancy? Transformed coat of arms, perhaps? Munificent dowry? Access to astonishing guest lists? Luxurious ongoing largesse?

Yes, something of a lottery, you see it so clearly, but after all a daughter is a modest wager for men of affairs like you – and some prizes are assured, none trivial. Do we have an understanding, then? I think we do. Shall we proceed?

Is she at hand?

My life as a Late Elizabethan

Alas my love
alas my lady
alas my queen
also sundry sirs and madams
also assorted soi-disant servants
of this our sovereign state (discuss)
not forgetting my captains sad and saucy
you condottieri in our killing fields
and indoor generalissimos
of hedge and mortgage
neither omitting a bow to equivocators
nor a tip of the hat to coney-catchers
cutpurses and mountebanks
ninnyhammers anthropophagi
bearers of false witness
and denizens of our cockpit
of state fireworks and plot
these thick rotundities
of falsehood panache
hugger mugger with your backroom stokers
of Rumour's many rancid tongues
and all you and all you
please tell me to where is it
our weary road will take us

Why man through the waning world
to your safe place
though the way runs
by indirect paths so go warily
for this is piss alley
know you not you tread

the banks of the shit brook
heed the concealed entrance at wideboy
corner (the one you can always cut)
the climb climb climb pant up nob hill
though the way is slippery there
and the underclass underpass
that craves wary walking
before we turn down dog-whistle drive
brimful of such solid model citizenry

So you will be calm there sir
we are cherished in our zones of protection
we are fully functional in our conservation areas
inside the triangle at the intersections
of checkpoint crossing of searchlight way
and barbed wire strand
with hardly a murmur from migrant piazza
and none at all from cemetery view
except the lapping of the sea
the lapping ever warmer ever nearer
ever more freighted with the desperate

And never ask
to what purpose are we
waiting inside our suburbs
inside our grid plans
never put the question
for waiting **is** the purpose
in and of itself that keeps us
in cut-throat business as usual
convoys of ransacked provender
beguiling the times till we can say
now comes in our special providence
in a downfall of sparrows

And if reports are carried
from poor desiccating shires
that the fields are choking
woodland has filled with absence
moorland is black and burning
and all the poor Toms go to it
rehearsing their sans everything
and if from other further scenes
of our heritage rape and rifling
we hear of golden lands gone to dust
vexed by flight and slaughter

We can say we do say
just tall tales from travellers
just axes to grind breastplates to burnish
destabilisation mythologies to spin
just misery memoir prequels

We can say we say
while there is honey still and tea
nothing to do with us sir

My lives in the gloaming

Again that time of day, end of another light shift, all detail and distance laid aside. To be unfinished differently tomorrow. Drowsy, then awake to the shirr of a flickerbook, clack of a roulette wheel slowing, stopping – who are you to be, come back to yourself at this hour?

1. This one, perhaps, sitting back, glass in hand, swirling the words around. *Gloaming*: let's see, you're getting *glow, gleam, glimmer*. A philologist? Or someone else may be gravely waiting: *loom, gloom, loam*. An undertaker? *Crépuscule*: are you getting pancakes or black mourning?

2. Another possibility for you. This one seems to be working in a respectable genre: writing home from the frontier ramparts at dusk. Expect wistfulness, ennui. *Nothing much happened again today. I miss you.* What threatens this literary tradition is the lack of messengers. Where it falls down is in the basic requirement that home needs to be still there.

3. Today's last confessed sin just dropped in the box provided, inscribed in your usual scrofulous script legible only to God. Is it wrong to be glad you've reached your quota and can put the pen down for the day? Well, yes, it is – so you'll need to write that down. You'll need to waste a bit of candle to see the extra scrap of paper to write it down. And you'll need to write that down. And you seem to have allowed yourself to run culpably short of ink. And… a long night in prospect, then.

4. There's your cue. It's time to get onstage again. Your character, who's made a few missteps, is getting near the end of his story, but can you remember what comes after *light thickens/and the crow makes wing to the rooky wood*?

5. Backsliding to dictatorship: it's not all bad news. You, comrade poet, and your muse have just about had enough of these aimless evenings, the anaemic wine of freedom, the dearth of good whispering sessions as the light gutters; now you'll be able to get back to your tried and trusted old style. You always know where you are with code and fable.

6. The light's lit. White shines through the holes in your official lighthouse keeper's sweater. Sitting inside a thousand beset granite tons, you're riveted by the new tremors in the whisky bottle.

7. You've been strict, you've told the children: don't, just don't, when the sun's going down, take that little path into the forest, no matter how the leaves shine in the last stray rays or how aromatically the evening perfumes rise. And quite right too. And here you are now, at just such an hour, pulling on your boots.

8. Disconcerting, the ride home at dusk, when you find a strange woman downstream from your house, scrubbing clothes. Your clothes. This will only happen once.

9. A new novel. You can't be bothered reading it. A new sweater. Save it for colder nights. A new notebook. You opened it and waited while the light dimmed. You're waiting, new pen in hand. Will wait.

10. Before getting as far as your face, after capturing the sumptuous detail of the collar and even the bunch of asparagus, that glaucous gleam so like Italian majolica, hmmm, yes – your self-portrait just ran our of light.

11. In the morgue by the Seine, they're lighting the candles. What's the betting you won't be able to find your body today either?

12. A good time to be working out what to do with the rest of your life. Assuming you've remembered which life it is. A good time to deliver your final report to yourself, stamped **For your eyes only**. Not a good time for your parents to emerge from their secret panel with wisdom to share, but here it comes anyway. *Ah widnae dae that if ah wis you, son.*

13. After a hard day working at the marble, you're peering down at the floor to see which of these shadowy chips is actually the block.

14. Are you dressing too young or too old? The dim mirror, unhelpfully, thinks both. The mirror also ventures the opinion that you most likely have ten – one zero – years left, maximum. Worrying enough; but of course, on reflection, coming from a mirror, could that really mean zero one years left?

15. Crepuscular, too, in the labyrinth. A man, a hero even, could lose faith in the possibility of the right turning. And if it's there it'll vanish soon anyway. Feeling your way any further becomes unthinkable, so you sit, back to the wall. Just you: true labyrinth, true monster.

16. A worrying hour in the memory palace. Something's been taken while your back was turned. There's an empty plinth. What was on it? A vase? A bust? A terrestrial globe? And what was it there to remind you of? Will you really have to launch into a full inventory of the corridor, including the animal heads and the second-rate art? Or if you go for a little stroll, might it mysteriously be restored, no questions asked?

17. On the evening of the adventure of the rest of your life – all planned and ticketed, lists checked and double-checked, case packed, clothes left out for the morning, an early supper picked at – your attempt to relax before bed is undermined by the

suspicion that well down the road tomorrow you'll be patting your pockets, knowing, just knowing that something (what? what?) will still be on the kitchen table.

18. In a moment you'll get up, descend to the dark basement and stop at the door of the room the music's coming from. Nothing to worry about; it's only your parents' vinyl record appreciation society, gleefully listening as Sir Harry Lauder gives them his *Roaming in the gloaming.* You'll be welcome.

My life with the critics

'My My My Life'? The stammering note sounded in the title is alas too predictive of the overflow of eager inability to articulate found within. Mr Paterson just needs a little kind assistance, a King's Speech (as it were) treatment for the flustered imagination, and all will flow more smoothly and (who knows) more impressively. Meantime, hands off the keyboard, Mr P!

Thurso Atom

Mrs Heather Wishart and Mrs Isobel Gault went shopping last Tuesday (8th) in Perth, where among the books they failed to buy was Andrew Paton's 'My Mile High Life'. The scones in the Dunsinane Tearoom were judged 'awfully satisfactory'.

Auchterarder Intelligencer

Read all about it! Fucking terrible collection!

Leith Literary Review

The smouldering heap throws off some sparks of native wit still, and one can only regret what great things might have been done had the author – at a vulnerable and unreflective age – not been seduced by the trans-border mirage of adventures with regularly replenished bank deposits, freethinking in humid boudoirs and gaudy acts of worship, happy hours, roads less travelled, regional cheeses, spinsters cycling a wee bit the worse for drink through misty meadows to evensong, to say nothing of those modishly alleged cellular urgings to widen the gene pool…

The West Lothian Presbyter

Is it poetry? Is it prose? We asked around. Nobody knows!

Borders Balladeer

Work so lacking the smack of firm control – be it editorial, be it authorial – sorely needs, for its own sake, a firm but well-intentioned correction, with every hope of a straight, clean-limbed narrative ensuing. As readers of this organ will appreciate, a little sharp pain and short-term throbbing soon gives way to the bracing sense of virtue re-booted.

Lochgelly Leathercraft

Great stuff. Try to fit in a few pages in bed to increase your chances of a quiet night. Indeed, you may feel that the author has already done your sleep-walking for you.

Kyles of Bute Somnambulist

Beware, Mr Paterson! The Stornoway Puffin has its eye on you!

Stornoway Puffin

www.ingramcontent.com/pod-product-compliance
Lightning Source LLC
Chambersburg PA
CBHW020218090426

42734CB00008B/1118